Copyright © 2013 by Samuel T. Schoemann

All rights reserved. No part of this publication may be reproduced, distributed, or transmitted in any form or by any means, including photo-copying, recording, or other electronic or mechanical methods, without the prior written permission of the publisher, except in the case of brief quotations embodied in critical reviews and certain other noncommercial uses permitted by copyright law. For permission requests, write to the publisher, addressed "Attention: Permissions Coordinator," at the address below.

Manual Press
12011 Goshen Avenue #305
Los Angeles, CA 90049 - U.S.A.

Edited by: Molly Schoemann

Book design & layout: Paul Takizawa/www.topaz4.com

ISBN: 978-0-615-81680-7

Ordering Information: Quantity sales. Special discounts are available on quantity purchases by corporations, associations, and others. For details, contact the publisher at the address above. Orders by U.S. trade bookstores and wholesalers. Please contact Manual Press: Tel: (310) 709-2194 or visit www.swimminginlakeme.com

First edition printing May 2013

SWIMMING IN LAKE ME

One Man's Journey of Discovery

Samuel Schoeman and Meredith McCann

DEDICATION

I dedicate this book to my amazing children Sam & Natalie - having Papa gone for six weeks was not easy for the two of you. I want to thank you two for all your love and understanding.

To my mom, Nancy; my dad, Albert; step-mom, Pamela; thank you so much for all the love understanding and support. I'm truly blessed to have you all in my life.

A special note of appreciation to my sister Molly Schoemann, for all her editorial help in getting this book done. I know, if I work hard enough, someday I might come close to being as talented a writer as she is (and hopefully not end my sentences with a preposition).

FORWARD

In the summer of 2012, after a divorce, a move, and a job loss, the author was a mess - the dream turned into the nightmare. To save his soul, he bought a 2000 Corvette convertible and embarked on a cross-country trip. The goal: Reflect on where he'd been and get a reality check on where he was going. This is his journey, a six-week inner expedition from California to Maine. The following are notes, pictures, and observations from his 6000 miles on the road and even some travel tips for those looking to take a similar drive. Ultimately, it was a time of insight, reflection, and find out what it means to go Swimming In Lake Me.

Journal Entry: July 2, 2012

OBSTACLES ARE NOT TRAGEDIES

SO, ABOUT 100 MILES out of Phoenix, truly in the middle of nowhere, I look down at my gas gauge and it's on empty. Only moments before I had just under half a tank and now, the needle is resting on the little pin! I will never forget the fear that hit me...running out of gas in the desert?! Only a few hours into my journey and I was going to die before the end of day one. I was by myself, in the middle of nowhere, in a car I knew little about - cue the circling vultures. I figured in 24 hours they would need dental records to identify my rotting carcass. It felt like the worst case scenario. Now granted, I was in a black car with the top down for 3 hours straight - essentially, with the hot wind, I was in a convection oven on wheels. And perhaps, given my "slightly" emotional state, I wasn't thinking completely clearly. But still, I thought the car would die at any moment and the panic felt overwhelming.

About 10 shaky, white knuckle miles down the road, I found a gas station in Buckeye, AZ - I got out and as I was filling up (and hoping it would only take about 10 gallons - meaning it was the gauge and not a leak in the tank / fuel system) a very sweet lady came up to me and asked if I was able to stay cool with the top down? We talked and I told her about my gas predicament. As she walked away to go pay for her gas she wished me good luck and God bless. Sure enough, the car only took 10 gallons, so it was the gauge after all. And sure enough, when I started her up, the gauge went right back to full. For some reason, it was really important for me to tell this lady I was OK, so I waited till she came out of the station. I told her what was up and she said she wanted ME to know she was going to say a prayer for me. Given the stress of the situation, I kinda lost it in front of her, but thanks to the polarized sunglasses, I don't think she saw my tears.

What I realized driving back to the freeway was that I HAVE NO CONTROL over life and that if the car is going to break down, then it's going to break down! Obstacles are not tragedies, and fears are in my head. I've grown up with little faith, in myself, others, God, etc. Fear is nature's early warning system, but for me, it takes hold and won't let go sometimes. It also reinforces my self doubt. When the gauge showed empty, my fear was on full - I will die here; or, if I survive, I will never sell this car because no one will ever buy it with a broken gas gauge; or, if I get to the gas station, some marauding band of Arizona biker hicks will be waiting there, sense my weakness and torture and kill me.

Seriously, all this over a temperamental gas gauge?

Sam Schoemann
July 2 near Los Angeles

It's late and I'm doing my final packing and hitting the road bright and early tomorrow. So far, the toughest thing was to say goodbye to Sammy and Natalie. My first stop: having breakfast with Brad Vettese in Palm Desert. Brad and I had coffee not too long ago and I scribbled some words on a napkin: "Purpose" and "Life's Work?" – that napkin traveling cross-country with me as well. Then off to Phoenix to spend a few days with my childhood friend, Chris Sabbarese.

Like · Comment · Share   👍 6 👎 10

THE SONG REMEMBERS WHEN

Music is incredibly transformative - Not only can it transport you back in time; it can also resurrect feelings of those moments. Burn those CD's, load up that iPod, this is your trip and YOU get to play DJ and create a soundscape as accompaniment. You will be surprised that music can be a salvation. They say that great art comes from a place of transition or conflict; trust me, eight hours on a highway in the middle of nowhere and you will be amazed at how you will suddenly be identifying with lyrics that only seemed like words the first 100 times you listed.

Journal Entry: July 7, 2012

REPAIR THE CORE…

AS I WAS DRIVING over the Rockies, I got scared. It started innocently enough. If there's one thing a Vette does well, it is drive over mountains. When you have 350+ horsepower, you have an engine that easily motors up any long ascent. Couple that with one of the best-handling cars ever to come out of Detroit, and you have a machine that carves up turns like a Thanksgiving turkey. NOBODY could stay with me - and it seemed that all was well in my teenage, "Speed Racer" fantasy; BUT, as we all know, in life a little rain must fall. And it did, a lot. Here's the downside to a Corvette in the rain; besides the fact you're practically sitting on the ground, the car has ZERO ground clearance underneath the vehicle. You hit a puddle and there's no place for the water to go. In the rain, my nice racing fantasy was reduced to "just keep her on the road…"

Anyway, there were a few times where I would be next to another vehicle and the wash from their tires would literally blind me to where I had zero visibility. Honestly, (and I'm not trying to be melodramatic) I was scared. You're driving along and then suddenly, you can't see AND you start hydroplaning: sheer fear. Fuck, this wasn't in the brochure!

OK - I made it through safe and sound. As it sank in, I flashed back to 25 years ago, when I was in a similar situation driving from Maine to Boston, in a horrific rainstorm on the Mass Pike – and I loved it! Zero visibility meant testing my skill, my mettle; I can still hear myself saying, "Bring it on!" Sure, I was a stupid kid (probably with a small death wish), but I wonder now, what the hell happened to me? Has life slowly crippled me? Am I a shell of the man I was? I desperately want to be that kid again, who is excited to NOT know what's right in front of me.

Here's the metaphor: I realized I need to live life from the inside out, not the outside in. To me, when you live life from the inside out - you're strong and centered; no matter what happens, you can hold it up against that "core" inside you and just know it will be OK. Over the past 25 years, I've lived life from the outside in, I've let the fears, disappointments, failures, mistakes, define who I am to me, and that core has been chipped away at badly. Part of this journey, this trip, this "long swim in lake me," is to repair my core.

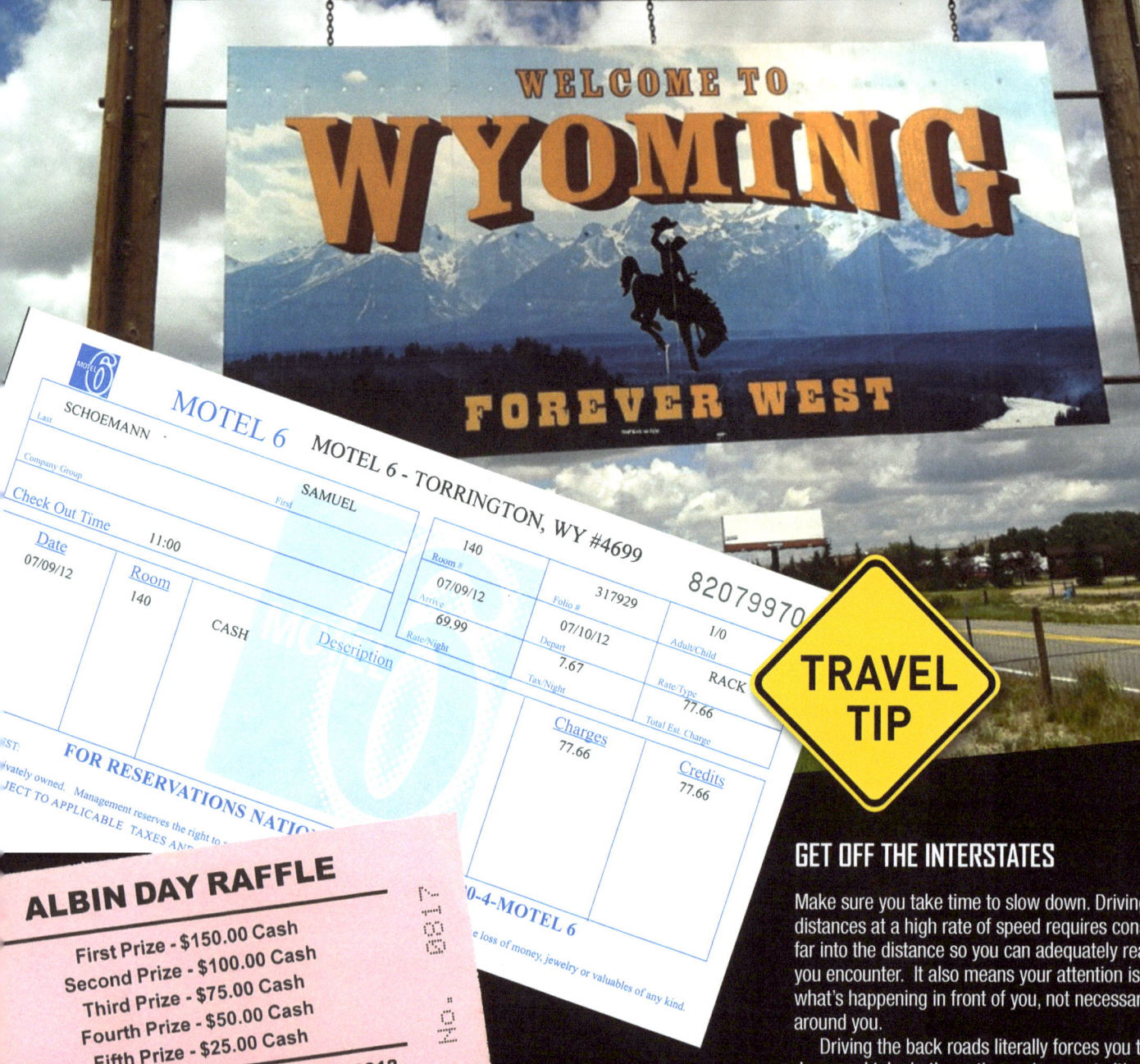

GET OFF THE INTERSTATES

Make sure you take time to slow down. Driving long distances at a high rate of speed requires constant focus far into the distance so you can adequately react to what you encounter. It also means your attention is trained on what's happening in front of you, not necessarily what's around you.

Driving the back roads literally forces you to slow down and take in the entire environment. It's an important exercise because it will push you to examine life on the periphery. In life as in nature, there are very few straight lines. Staying off the interstates will allow you to embrace the subtlety and nuances of the journey while deemphasizing the destination.

Journal Entry: July 10, 2012

THE CLICHÉ...

AS I'M TOOLING DOWN the road, out in the middle of nowhere, I see a skydiver, parachute open, drifting down to earth. Watching his circling descent, I was struck by the old cliché - this person will "land on their feet." I've never been a big, "the universe will give you what you need" kind of guy, but in that fleeting moment, I took it as a sign that I too will land on my feet.

This "sign" also brought to the forefront one of my all time fears: sky-diving. It's got all the things that scare me the most: a terrifying fear of heights and a fear of flying that I've battled with for 30 years and my reoccurring plane crash nightmare. So, ladies and gentlemen, this week somewhere in the Northwestern states where I will be meandering for the next 5 days, I will be jumping out of a plane.*

I'm beginning to realize that life is about relishing those times of absolute uncertainty, of having faith. I had a boss who would (wisely) say, you have to be uncomfortable in life because if you're comfortable, you're not changing. Of course, easier said than done, but who knows, until you leap out of the plane.

*Still working to muster the courage.

TRAVEL TIP

GET SOME PERSPECTIVE – START BY BEING HUMBLED

On your journey, take in the scenery, the hills, the lakes, the mountains, and the dirt by the side of the road and remember, all the natural scenery has been there for millions of years before you and will be there way past your grandchildren's, grandchildren. Our existence? A mere speck of sand on some long forgotten beach. While our issues may seem larger than life, they're actually insignificant in the grand scheme. I'm not saying what's going on has no bearing; it's just that having perspective can help decrease the weight.

Saturday, Jul 14,
National Theatre Live in London Pro

Frankenstein

Presented by: M.C. Ginsberg
221 E. Washington Street
www.englert.org
319-688-2653

General
2402586

General Admission

Englert — It All Happens Here — www.englert.org — NO REFUNDS NO EXCHANGES

National Park Service
U.S. Department of the Interior
Mount Rushmore National Memorial
Keystone, South Dakota

Mount Rushmore

"... let us place there, carved high, as close to heaven as we can, the words of our leaders, their faces, to show posterity what manner of men they were. Then breathe a prayer that these records will endure until the wind and rain alone shall wear them away."

—Gutzon Borglum, Mount Rushmore Sculptor, 1930

The granite portraits of George Washington, Thomas Jefferson, Theodore Roosevelt, Abraham Lincoln represent the birth, growth, development and preservation of the nation.

When sculptor Gutzon Borglum looked upon the knobby, cracked face of Mount Rushmore in the Black Hills of South Dakota, he saw a vision of four United States presidents carved into the mountain. In 1927, with the help of over 400 workers and several influential politicians, Borglum began carving a memorial to the history of America. Today Mount Rushmore is host to around three million visitors each year from across the country and around the world.

Interpretive Ranger Programs

Mount Rushmore park rangers offer a variety of interpretive programs throughout the summer season including Ranger Walks, Studio Talks and Evening Programs. Cultural programs and hands-on activities for children are also offered throughout the summer. Please inquire at the information desk for exact times. An audio tour and Junior Ranger Programs are available year-round to help visitors of all ages learn about many aspects of the park.

Journal Entry: July 13, 2012

YOU DON'T HAVE A GLASS JAW

I WAS RUNNING LATE to see my friends in Iowa City and didn't want to show up on their doorstep at 2am. So, I made a beeline to Des Moines and headed downtown to have an adult beverage and maybe chat up a lady or two. I figured I'd have a few drinks, get back on the road and find a place to crash for a while along the way to Iowa City.

As luck would have it, I sparked up a conversation with a local kid (OK mid 20's, but everyone in their 20's feels like a kid to me). We had the typical guy talk about life, women, booze, etc. He was a local farm boy, and as we talked about growing up, he told me about having close friends whose families had cabins, lake houses, boats, etc. For me, being a city kid growing up in Manhattan, it sounded idyllic. Then he said something telling - he told me that when he got to college he and his friend used to go to bars and get into fights and THEY LOVED IT. To me, this was a total disconnect - I'm Mr. Gun Control, words not fists, can we all get along, urban pacifist. Beating the crap out of each other? Really? He said to me, "Sam, the best part about getting hit in the face is that you realize, very quickly, that you don't have a glass jaw (a glass jaw is an old boxing adage; a fighter with a glass jaw is someone who can't take a punch). When you get knocked down, it hurts, but you also get to get back up, dust yourself off, and get back into the fight."

Thinking back to that innocuous conversation, I realized there were many times when I didn't get back up. Life hit me square in the face and I lost faith in myself, or worse, I lost the ability to simply get up and put one foot in front of the other. It's a terrifying feeling to see only darkness. This kid, in his one little way, held a mirror to my face and let me see that I don't have a glass jaw. There have been a few times on this trip when I didn't think I could get back up; yet each time I was hit with fear or despair - crossing the Rockies or a busted gas gauge - I didn't cave; I proved I could take a punch.

Journal Entry: July 18, 2012

IF YOU HAD EVERYTHING, NOTHING WOULD BE SPECIAL

ONE THING I DID NOT anticipate on my trip was a massive heat wave and subsequent drought that gripped the Midwest during my journey. I made the drive from Iowa, met up with an old friend and had a lovely, alcohol-infused evening. It was midnight and my next stop, Madison, WI, was a good 5 hour drive away. Knowing I was in no condition to drive, I grabbed my pillow from the trunk and attempted to get comfortable for a sleep-off. Even at midnight, it was hot – Midwestern drought hot. I tried everything, tossing and turning in the Vette seat to get relaxed and grab shuteye, but it was not happening. I was drunk, hot and miserable. It was so hot, I eventually opened the car door and literally spilled out on the lawn next to where I was parked. Around 5 hours into this miserableness, I sobered up enough to get into my car and make the trek to Madison. Of the hundred plus hours I had spent on the road, this was by far the worst stretch.

Tired, sweaty, cranky and still hung-over, I arrived at my childhood Lisa Ferin's house. Seeing my condition, she ushered me to her guest bedroom. This I will never forget: when I got into the bed, it was the most comfortable bed I had EVER slept in in my life and I was out like a light. The fact that this was the greatest bed in the world struck me. How could this be? I've been fortunate enough to stay in some posh hotels with swanky sleeping arrangements. I consider myself a connoisseur in the ways of thread count, goose down and box springs. No offense, Lisa – but how could you have the single most comfy bed in the Western World?

The truth was obvious. The fact that I had had the worst sleeping arrangements the previous night confirmed that, when you go without, then you have it, you cherish it so much more. Was it the most comfortable bed? It sure felt like it when the night before you were sleeping on grass.

This one little incident illustrated to me that I take too much for granted. I've based my life on chasing things, and when you do that, it's easy to lose track of what's important. How in the world can I cherish my accomplishments if I can't enjoy the small victories along the way? Or review what didn't go my way not necessarily as failure but as recalibrating what was important?

It made me realize that contentment can be gleaned from what you have, NOT what you want, and that I need to truly appreciate what's in front of me, not what I think is over the horizon. Perhaps a building block to happiness is not having everything you thought was important because that way you can truly appreciate what you do have.

TALK MUCH - LISTEN MORE

Tell everyone what you're going through AND make sure to listen intently to their responses. You will find that the more you talk about your situation, the easier it is to objectively understand the events that led you there. Talk with the new friends you make on your journey - they don't know your back-story, so their feedback is based simply on the information you provide.

  Also, be frank with the good friends you visit on your journey. Remember, friends know you better than you may think and will provide powerful context to the situation. Ultimately your closest friends want you to be happy, so help them, help you.

Journal Entry: July 20, 2012

TREAT EVERYONE LIKE A FRIEND

MY JOURNEY HAS GIVEN ME a great excuse to reconnect with friends and loved ones around the country. Some of the folks I've known for 30+ years but haven't seen them in as nearly as long. (Granted, Facebook has a lot to do with that).

So, I began to think about it - why was I so blessed with friends? I came across a posting on Facebook:

"The 7 Greatest Real Bill Murray Stories Ever Told"

The upshot of the article was that even for someone who's reached the pinnacle of fame and fortune, Mr. Murray's true likability lies in the fact that he treats everyone like a friend. The seven stories bore that out.

Look, I'm no Bill Murray (which, frankly would make a great book title) but this resonated with me; the more I thought about it, the more I realized: I easily connect with people because I consider everyone I meet a friend.

Direct social interaction, especially meeting new people, can be tough. My sense is we all get a little too caught up in how we present to the outside world. Subsequently, we're not 100% percent present when we interact with new people. Most human beings desperately want to connect but we're conflicted – we don't want to be judged, we don't want to be slighted and most of all, we don't want to be hurt.

Think about the ease you have when talking with friends. It's as if the built-in defense mechanisms are downgraded a notch or two. Also, don't you feel like you have some "skin in the game" when talking to friends? You're engaged, interested, and want to be supportive.

So, I can honestly say I have something in common with Bill Murray (besides rugged good looks): I consider everyone a peer, and as such, I relate to people easily.

Funny, it should take a trip across the US and a random article to make me realize I truly enjoy connecting with people because I too simply treat everyone I meet as a friend.

HAVE FUN, BUT DON'T MAKE IT ABOUT FUN

You're on the road, on an emotional roller coaster, and blowing into town after town. I jokingly told my friends, "Want free booze? Say you bought a corvette and you're driving from California to Maine and you never have to buy another drink again." It's easy, in the state you're in to party and womanize, but that's not the reason you're on this journey. Have fun, but don't take your eye off the ball. This is about reflection, discovery and self realization, and that's tough to do when you have a drink in one hand and God only knows who in the other.

Journal Entry: July 26, 2012

THAT'S NOT "YOUR PATH"

ON MY WAY TO NEW YORK, I visited good friends who are very successful. They've attained both professional and personal achievement. Yet after our visit, I was left with a profound sense of the "Why Not Me's?" i.e. why didn't I have similar accomplishments? It wasn't jealousy, it was more a sense of failure: All things being equal, I wondered how come I never seemed to reach that level of success. And perhaps more importantly, why did I always have this need to compare myself to others?

So, here I was on the road thinking, "Why did I feel like a failure? Why am I saddened by the fact that I don't have what others have attained? Then, it literally hit me like a lightning bolt – Why? Simple: That wasn't my path!

While it might sound trite, life is the journey down YOUR path. Whenever we use external expectations to judge ourselves, it's a flawed exercise, because our path is completely individual.

It was one of the greatest senses of relief I've ever experienced. A great weight had been lifted. I realized that where I am in life and where I'm going really can't be compared to anyone else's journey – everyone has his or her own route in life. I'm on my path right now AND I'm right where I need to be. I suddenly felt comfortable, at ease and at peace with myself.

Sam Schoemann
July 16 near Saint Paul, MN via mobile

He/she who dies with the most friends wins.

Unlike · Comment   👍 7   💬 7

RETHINK, RELIVE, REBOOT

On the road, take time to review some of the defining moments that have forged your life and examine the events in terms of emotional impact. Start by recreating in your mind the context, the stakes, and the players; then think about how you reacted to the situation and would you change how you responded now?

Now is the time to benefit from wisdom and hindsight. Do some critical thinking, share it with others, and unlock some feelings. On the journey, it's just you and the road: Deal with it with an even hand - think of it in the third person - what kind of advice would you give yourself today? Most of all, be kind to yourself; give yourself permission to heal.

Journal Entry: August 3, 2012

I HURT MYSELF THE WORST

I'M ON THE ROAD and tears begin to flow. With hours to go to the next destination it begins to dawn on me that I'm the cause of all my pain; I hurt myself the worst AND I'm really good at it. I know how to pour the salt, pick the scab, picture the unthinkable, or drudge up something from the past to inflict personal punishment. So how did I get here?

As a child, my survival plan was to make everyone around me happy – essentially to put their emotional needs first. Early on, I was overwhelmed by circumstances that were simply beyond my control. I figured if I can put the world first and make everyone around me happy, then I too would be happy. In retrospect, not a bad plan when you're a five-year-old but one major flaw: try as you may, you can never make everyone happy – and of course I failed.

Here's the kicker – when I failed, I blamed myself, and thus, the personal punishment. If anyone around me was unhappy (regardless of the reason) then somehow it was my fault.

So I thought, "Now what? How in the world can I undo 40+ years of behavior?" I suspect the solution will emerge in my next book. But for now, I can be pragmatic: I look at personal change as steering an ocean liner. Big, big boats are really good at going in one direction, but trying to make a major course correction takes time and energy. That said, I know a small course adjustment now can lead to a big change in direction over time.

If anything, this journey has shed light on my need for external validation (and not blaming myself if I don't get it) and I consider this my first course correction in making lasting change.

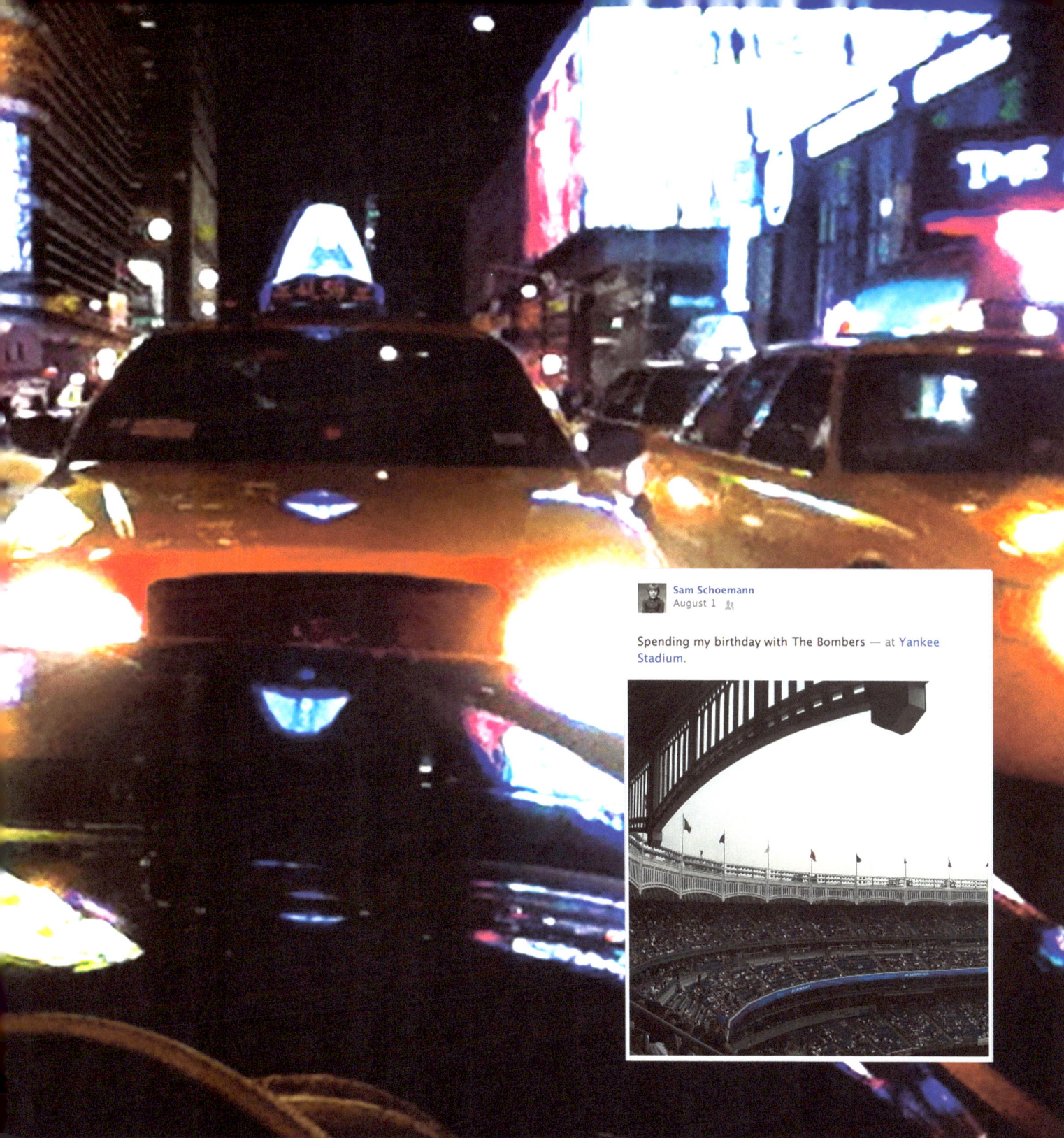

Journal Entry: August 10, 2012

PAR FOR THE COURSE

ON THE LAST DAY of my trip I went golfing with my Dad. I was excited to end the trip spending time with my father. He was undergoing treatment for prostate cancer, and while everything was going according to plan, I still felt the need to support him, considering how much he supported me during the dark days of my life. My Dad has always enjoyed golf, not that he played much, twice a year at most. But it was his thing and I wanted to be a part of it, if for no other reason than to share in one of his passions. We went to a PAR-3 course, which was just enough for both of us to handle. I wanted desperately to make a par on one hole and on the 14th hole, I had my shot. Off the tee, I hit a perfect 5 iron that split the green and landed a mere 20 feet from the cup. OK, 20 feet – just get it close and I can two putt it for par. Well, I got a case of the "Yipps" and laid it up to within 5 feet of the hole. NOW the pressure was on. As I addressed the ball, I literally thought, "If I miss this, my entire trip will be ruined." Really, that thought actually crossed my mind. Did I blow the putt? Of course, and in spectacular fashion. I stayed strong on the outside for my Dad but I was crying on the inside.

So we headed to the 15th tee and frankly, I was still shattered from my meltdown. My first shot bounced off a tree and landed in the cart path. I pitched the second shot onto the green but a good 50 feet from the pin. Lining up the putt this time, I felt no pressure and figured I would do my best to get it to the hole. Low and behold, I nailed that 50-foot putt for par! It struck me, what would it be like if I could have had that easiness with my first put? What was it inside me that I needed to put so much pressure on myself, and why do I picture failure as opposed to success? If life can sometimes feel like swimming upstream, why do I put boulders in my pockets?

For me, those boulders are fear. And my fear comes in many flavors: Fear of failure, of making a mistake, of not being perfect, of letting the world down, etc. The aggregate pressure of all that fear is extremely paralyzing.

What the golf experience made me realize was that the vast majority of that fear is strictly internal and more importantly, it's not accurate or rooted in reality. It's also given me a new perspective, the "life is a 50-foot putt" mantra. When I face a challenge, I can't worry about the outcome. All I can do is show up and take the next shot; eventually good things will happen.

TRAVEL TIP

ATTEND TO UNFINISHED BUSINESS

One of the amazing things you will find in reconnecting with those from your past is that you will get to relive your mutual history from a distinctly different point of view. What you will discover is your recollection might not be that accurate and what you've deemed important may not have had much impact on others. Make it a point to visit someone where there was a significant historical landmine - a jilted lover, a toxic friendship, or estranged relative. Now is the time to reconcile, because a festering wound only get worse over time. Remember, a lighter load gives you more strength.

FROM DAY ONE of the trip, there was only one certainty; when I got to my final destination I would sell the vette. I always considered "Ray" (as in Corvette Stingray) not just my sidekick but also a supporting character in the book. Was Ray the ultimate symbol of the preverbal midlife crisis? A cry for attention? A phallic emblem of male inadequacy? Sure (well maybe except the last one). Yet, in an ironic way, we were similar. Even with 75K on the odometer we still had a lot of life in the tank. Sure our paint was worn and interior a little torn, but together we still commanded a little respect on the road and a friendly wink or two.

In the end selling the car was my way of ending this chapter in my life. After all, Ray got me where I needed to be; to a place where I could start releasing the past and embrace the future. I will miss Ray for giving me the freedom of the open road and the sheer pleasure of owning a vehicle I would never even come close to testing its limits.

So, in closing and to everyone who reads this book, the one thing I know now: If you think your journey's over, it's only just begun...

Finally, in order of appearance, thanks to my friends and family I visited on this journey. You inspired me to write this book.

SWIMMING IN LAKE ME

U.S. TOUR SUMMER 2012

Brad Vettese	Palm Desert, CA	July 2
Chris Sabbarese	Phoenix, AZ	July 3
Wendy Lippman	Sedona, AZ	July 6
Tom Anthony	Denver, CO	July 7
David Busch	Iowa City, IA	July 13
Claudia Rothchild	St. Paul, MN	July 15
Lisa Ferin	Madison, WI	July 16
Paul Sloboda	Carbondale, IL	July 18
Kelley Parmenter	Louisville, KY	July 20
Molly Schoemann	Garner, NC	July 21
Kim Herring	Cary, NC	July 26
Michael Halloran	Richmond, VA	July 27
Sarah Schoemann	Brooklyn, NY	July 28
Craig Parks	New York, NY	July 30
Janis Brody	New York, NY	July 31
Fred Melamed,	Montauk, NY	August 2
Fitch Bullard	Guilford, CT	August 3
Polly Corn	Boston, MA	August 4
Kristen Vermilyea	Portsmouth, NH	August 5
Kirk Wolfinger	Belfast, ME	August 6
Albert Schoemann	Cape Cod, MA	August 10

www.ingramcontent.com/pod-product-compliance
Lightning Source LLC
Chambersburg PA
CBHW041538040426
42446CB00002B/144